WINDSURFING

PICTURE LIBRARY
WINDSURFING

Norman Barrett

Franklin Watts

London   New York   Sydney   Toronto

© 1987 Franklin Watts

First published in Great Britain 1987 by
Franklin Watts
12a Golden Square
London W1R 4BA

First published in the USA by
Franklin Watts Inc
387 Park Avenue South
New York
N.Y. 10016

First published in Australia by
Franklin Watts
14 Mars Road
Lane Cove
2066 NSW

UK ISBN: 0 86313 511 0
US ISBN: 0-531-10354-4
Library of Congress Catalog Card
Number 86-51227

Printed in Italy

Designed by
Barrett & Willard

Photographs by
All-Sport
All-Sport Vandystadt
N.S. Barrett Collection
Steve Maxted
Mistral
Nabisco
Jon Nicholson
Timex

Illustration by
Rhoda & Robert Burns

Technical Consultant
Clive Boden

Contents

Introduction

Windsurfing is a new sport, yet in just a few years it has become one of the world's most popular outdoor activities. Windsurfers are seen on lakes and in oceans in all parts of the world.

Windsurfers enjoy the sport as a pastime, from sailing gently on calm waters to "funboarding" on waves. There are also various competitions.

△ Windsurfing on calm water under a warm sun has become a popular leisure activity offshore around the world.

Windsurfers, or boardsailors, take part in world championships and a class for windsurfers was included in the 1984 Olympics. There are also speed competitions and endurance records.

In a branch of the sport called freestyle, competitors are judged on various tricks. Funboarding is also competitive, with course racing, slalom and wave riding.

△ An expert windsurfer, or funboarder, jumps out of the surf under a blue Hawaiian sky.

The sailboard

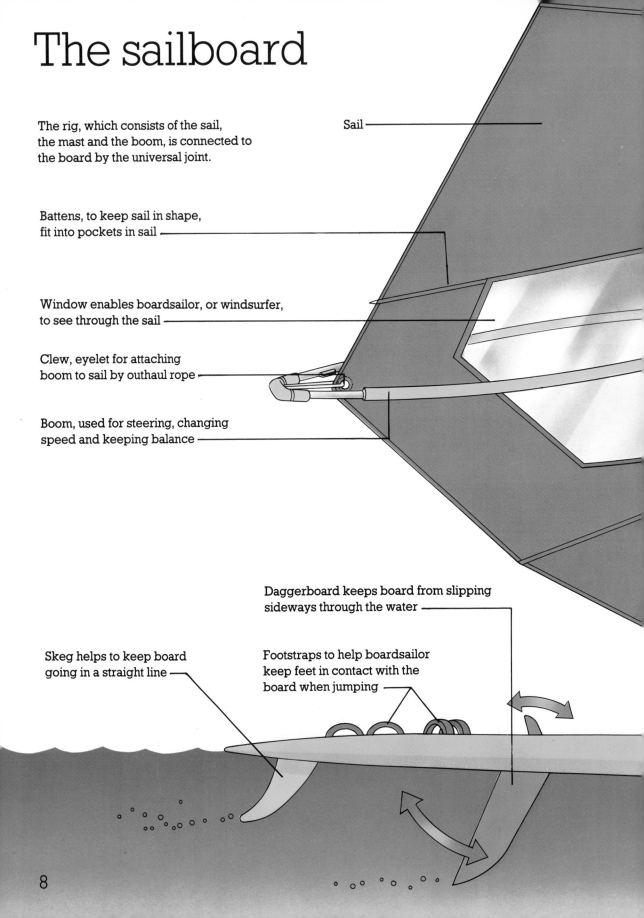

The rig, which consists of the sail,
the mast and the boom, is connected to
the board by the universal joint.

Sail

Battens, to keep sail in shape,
fit into pockets in sail

Window enables boardsailor, or windsurfer,
to see through the sail

Clew, eyelet for attaching
boom to sail by outhaul rope

Boom, used for steering, changing
speed and keeping balance

Daggerboard keeps board from slipping
sideways through the water

Skeg helps to keep board
going in a straight line

Footstraps to help boardsailor
keep feet in contact with the
board when jumping

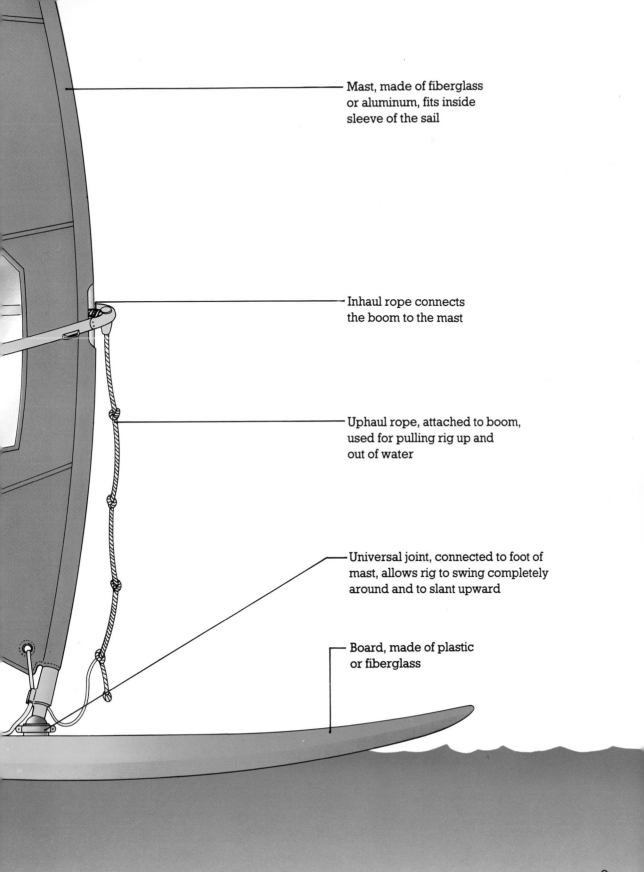

Mast, made of fiberglass
or aluminum, fits inside
sleeve of the sail

Inhaul rope connects
the boom to the mast

Uphaul rope, attached to boom,
used for pulling rig up and
out of water

Universal joint, connected to foot of
mast, allows rig to swing completely
around and to slant upward

Board, made of plastic
or fiberglass

Windsurfing for fun

The windsurfer rig is a simple little craft. There is no rudder, and it is steered by means of the sail. The sailor supports the rig by holding the boom.

You steer a windsurfer rig by tilting the sail. There is a correct position of the sail for the course you want to steer, depending on the direction of the wind.

▽ Young people and their dog have fun on a board. But it would be dangerous for them to sail any distance from the beach. Windsurfers must be good swimmers and wear lifejackets.

You can have great fun windsurfing whether you are in a group or on your own.

△ Dozens of windsurfers set out from the beach at the start of a race. Win or lose, they are sure to enjoy themselves.

◁ A lone windsurfer enjoys the peace of a wooded shore.

11

Learning to windsurf is not difficult. Like skating or riding a bike, when you have mastered the basic skills of balance and control, you never forget them.

Before learning to sail, you have to be able to raise the rig from the water. You do this with the uphaul rope. This requires balance and the ability to make the best use of your strength.

▽ The knots in the uphaul rope are used to pull the rig out of the water. A wet sail can be very heavy, and good balance is needed. You should always have an experienced windsurfer nearby when you are learning.

Traditional windsurfing boards are designed for light and moderate wind. Funboarding is an advanced type of windsurfing. Special boards are used and strong winds are necessary. Boards with flat bottoms are suitable for beginners because they are easier to sail. Racing boards have rounded bottoms. Funboards have footstraps so that the boardsailor can stay on the board even when going fast and jumping waves.

△ When you are jumping waves and flying through the air on a funboard, you need footstraps. Otherwise, you will fall off the board.

13

Racing

Standard windsurf racing is called triangle racing, because it is held on a triangular course like that used in yacht racing.

In funboard racing, there is less upwind sailing. There are also slalom races for funboards, on a zigzag course around marker buoys.

In "one-design" classes, such as the Mistral Superlight, competitors race on identical boards.

△ A "Le Mans" start to a funboard race. At the signal, the competitors race across the beach carrying their boards and rigs, and get going in the water as fast as they can.

△ Rounding a marker
buoy in a windsurfer
race. Buoys are used to
mark a racing course.
There are penalties for
touching the buoys or
not rounding them
properly.

▷ The 1984 Olympic
windsurfer class, the
Windglider, sailed by
the silver-medalist Scott
Steele of the United
States.

15

Freestyle

Freestyle windsurfing is like gymnastics on sailboards. The competitors go through set routines, performing tricks and other movements.

A freestyle display includes balancing feats on the board and with the rig, and special maneuvers in the water. Judges award points.

▷ A freestyle competitor turns the board on edge for a railriding trick, sailing with the feet on the upturned edge of the board.

▽ A head dip (left) and doing the splits while railriding (right).

Funboarding

Funboarding is a sport of high-speed thrills, spectacular flying jumps and split-second maneuvers through the waves and surf.

There are many types of funboards. Most are designed for sailing in strong winds of about 15 knots (17 mph or 28 km/h).

Funboarders sail in races, in wave-riding and jumping contests or just for the sheer excitement of it.

▽ Short funboards move fast through the waves and give more maneuverability in steering. They are at their best in strong winds of 15 knots or more. They are called "sinkers," because they tend to sink if the wind drops.

△ The start of a race. One funboarder has made a very good start and has taken a clear lead, while others are still struggling off the beach.

▷ Rounding a mark in a funboard race.

◁ The spectacular
side of funboarding,
jumping over the waves
in heavy surf.

A funboarder needs
to be able to "read" the
waves, to know which
ones to ride and which
ones to jump. Jumping is
not as difficult as it
looks. The funboarder
must find a suitable
wave from which to
launch the board and
then get up enough
speed before sailing up
the face of the wave and
"taking off."

The top wave-sailors
can perform upside-
down jumps and even
loops while in the air,
and then land smoothly
without spinning out of
control.

The thrills of funboarding, on boards old and new, are illustrated on these pages. Whether speeding over the water, leaping like salmon over the surf or even falling off, funboarders enjoy a great sport.

Other windsurfing sports

Variations of windsurfing have developed that can be enjoyed on and off the water.

Tandem windsurfng has its enthusiasts and there is even a three-man board called a "tridem."

By replacing the board with wheels, windsurfing rigs have been adapted for use on land. Runners can be used on ice, and skis or a special board can be used on snow.

▽ Tandem windsurfing gives boardsailors the pleasure of sailing with a companion. The different skills needed to operate a board with two sails must be learned by experience.

△ Some sailboards are designed purely for speed. These two boardsailors are taking part in speed trials. The average of several runs is taken to establish speed records.

◁ A combination of windsurfing and skiing skills is needed to operate this "ski-sailor." The mast is adapted to join the two skis together.

25

Landsurfers enjoy their sport on shallow sands.

"Landsurfing" is fast and furious. It can also be very dangerous. Coming off at high speed, especialy on a hard surface, might produce a violent landing, and landsurfers always wear helmets and protective padding. A bigger danger, perhaps, is being run over by another landsurfer's wheels.

The story of windsurfing

A sport is born

Windsurfing is a new sport, pioneered in the United States in the late 1960s. But it was in Europe, in the 1970s, that windsurfing first became popular.

There have been many arguments about who invented the sailboard. In 1982, an English court ruled that the inventor had been a 12-year-old British boy, Peter Chilvers, in 1958. Since that ruling, other claims have been made in other countries. But the board that first swept the world was the design called the Windsurfer. It was invented in California in 1968 by an American aeronautical engineer Jim Drake, together with his colleague Hoyle Schweitzer, who spread the idea around the world.

△ Schweitzer's original Windsurfer, a flat-bottomed board, has remained popular over the years.

The first boards

The first sailboards were flat-bottomed. Schweitzer's flatboard design is still used today, for both racing and recreational purposes, because flatboards are easy to learn on and to sail.

△ An illustration of over a hundred years ago shows how people controlled their movements on ice by maneuvering hand-held sails. It was a long time before this idea was adapted for use on water.

△ US freestyle stars Cheri, Susi and Lori Swatek. Freestyle developed as a competitive sport in the 1970s.

△ In the 1984 Olympics, at Los Angeles, windsurfing was introduced into the Games with the Windglider class.

△ The introduction of footstraps revolutionized windsurfing and led to the development of funboards.

Competition

As with most new sporting activities, windsurfing enthusiasts soon got together to compete in races. The first world championships were staged in 1973, and freestyle was included in 1977.

Boardsailing is the latest sport to be staged in the Olympics, in 1984, when the Windglider class was included as a yacht racing event.

Funboarding

A major advance in the sport was made in Hawaii in 1977 with the simple invention of footstraps, by windsurfer Larry Stanley. This gave boardsailors greater control at high speed and enabled them to ride waves, jumping out of surf

and landing without coming off the board. These "waveboards" soon led to the development of even faster boards – called funboards.

Funboarding – sailing in strong winds – soon became very popular. It developed as a separate sport, with its own world championships.

△ The first funboards, or waveboards, were short with square tails. They were developed for riding the waves in Hawaii.

Facts and records

Champions

The first Olympic boardsailing champion, in 1984, was Dutchman Stephan van den Berg. He also won five world titles (1979 to 1983).

The undisputed champion of the sport, however, is US star Robby Naish. He won his first world titles in the mid-1970s at the age of 14 and has dominated professional boardsailing for years.

△ Van den Berg (left) and Naish.

Speed and Endurance

Windsurfer Pascal Maka of France broke the world record for any sailing vessel in July 1986 with a speed of 38.86 knots (nearly 45 mph or 72 km/h).

In August 1986, British windsurfer Steve Maxted completed a marathon sailing session of 103 hours, 33 minutes and 33 seconds.

△ Marathon man – Steve Maxted.

△ The fastest – Pascal Maka.

Long-distance windsurfing

In 1986, French windsurfers Stephane Peyron and Alain Pichavant crossed the Atlantic in their tandem sailboard, from Africa to the West Indies, in a record 24 days, 12 hours and 5 minutes.

△ Peyron and Pichavant.

Glossary

Battens
Strips of plastic or fiberglass that fit into pockets in the sail to keep its shape.

Boardsailing
Another word for windsurfing.

Boom
A windsurfer has a double boom, sometimes called the wishbone. It is used to control the sail.

Buoy
A distinctly shaped stationary float used for marking out a racing course.

Daggerboard
A removable fin that projects underneath the board and stops sideways slip.

Freestyle
Performing tricks on the board.

Funboard
A board designed for sailing in strong winds.

Le Mans start
A running start off the beach.

Railriding
A freestyle trick, sailing the board on its edge.

Rig
The sail, mast and boom.

Sailboard
The board.

Skeg
A small plastic fin near the tail of the board that helps to keep it on course, especially in windy conditions.

Slalom
A race with a zigzag course.

Tandem
A board with two sails, for sailing by two people.

Triangle racing
Racing on a standard windsurfing course, as for Olympic sailing events.

Universal joint
The linkage connecting the mast to the board and allowing it to be tilted and swiveled.

Uphaul
Rope used to pull the rig out of the water.

Wave riding
Funboard contest in which judges award points for tricks performed on the waves.

Index